GARY,

DO WHAT

CAROL SAYS!

Ruf Havens

Published by Nice Dog Press, Bloomington, Illinois 61704.

Nice Dog Press books may be purchased in bulk for business, fundraising or promotional use. Please call (800) 642-3364 for more information.

Printed in the United States of America.

Everything I Needed To Know I Learned From MY WIFE!

by Rex Havens

Nice Dog Press

To Sarah:

My favorite and most patient teacher, and the only one I ever kissed. You make the sun rise and my heart dance. OK, you make the sun rise. Even with your love, I still can't dance.

- Rex

Table Of Contents

Rex Havens

Foreword

To Men

It takes dignified courage to admit being outmatched, but we must summon the valor to hail our conquerors. If it gives comfort, remember that we admire history's great generals not only for battles won but sometimes for knowing when to quit. Fear not, however, for when certain defeat is honestly faced, a calm, inner peace descends, warming the soul, control is released, one is bathed in serenity, and transported to a place of bliss. Just like freezing to death.

To Women

Most men beyond the age of 40 know the score. We know this is an Olympics where we scored no medals, a four-game World Series, a roseless Derby with a most unpleasant view. Remember only that, true to our sports ethic, we continue to admire good winners, those who do not gloat, those who are generous in victory, those willing to magnanimously offer hope to all for next season. However slim, leave us some hope for next year. It's what gets us through a long, cold winter. Please, don't let us freeze to death.

Rex Havens

Chapter #1

I'm Having the Time of My Wife!

Rex Havens

I was a young man once. It didn't work out.

But I was gloriously young, full of myself, confident, and believed fervently, as young men do, that it was a "man's world." I see it today, reflected in the eyes of bold young bucks, embarking on manhood, convinced it is their destiny to control the world and rule all they see. To those young men I offer two thoughts: One, I admire your optimism. Two, grow up.

Don't take my word for it, though, young lads. Go out there into the world, struggle, fight! Maybe _you_ are the chosen one. Maybe you are going to succeed where 12 billion men before you have failed.

Then again, maybe not. But give it your best shot.

But on behalf of all the other men who no longer cling to their boyish dream, I'd like to take this opportunity to speak to the women. Now I can only speak as a man, it is the handicap I was born with. But I offer this to you earnestly, in the spirit of healing, I say it with love, honor, respect, affection and all good things, and I think I speak for many men in the world when I say to you . . . honest to goodness . . . we have . . . . truly . . . . tried!   We have _tried_ so very hard to understand you. OK, as best we can with our tiny, underdeveloped little brains. But every time in my life I thought maybe I understood one, small itty-bitty truth about you women, I think you all call a meeting. You take a vote, you change the rule. You don't tell the man in your life, because that would take the sport right out of it. You leave it up to him to figure out for himself, individually, if he can, sometimes he does, more often he does not - pfft! - the game goes on.

After all these years, it comes down to only two things about men and women which I know are always true. There are only two things I can count on, they're always there for me:

#1 - I'm a man.

#2 - I'm sorry!

Because I have very bad news for the men of America.   Battle of the Sexes?   I'm so very sorry . . . . but it's over . . . and we lost! I believe I can hear the voices of the women of America saying, "Son of a gun! One of 'em finally gets it! Now we're gonna have to call a meeting."

But take heart men, we have nothing to be ashamed of. We put up a long, hard, valiant fight . . . and came in second. That's not so bad. After all, second is almost first. When you think about it, we did pretty well. We beat every gender out there, except that one.

From my own valiant fight, I ultimately came to learn that marriage is a democracy - One Woman, One Vote.

I'm told it's not this way everywhere. I understand there are women in the world who are docile, subservient, women who hang on their husband's every word, and treat him like a god. I have never met any of these women - because I live in North America.

And as it turns out, North America is not the ideal environment for the adult male ego to be nurtured and thrive. The male ego. I know it can be a trying and frustrating adversary for many women. I'd like to tell you about the day I lost mine forever.

I was about 40 years old, sitting in my living room, and I was having one of those moments when you count your blessings and appreciate how good life has been to you. Now I don't live in a mansion by any means, but as I sat there, I felt life had been exceedingly kind to me, and I was feeling grateful that day for what I had, my wonderful family, a comfortable home. And as I looked at the things around me - a lifetime-to-date of living room furniture, decorations and mementos - I suddenly realized for the first time - it hit me like a bolt - that of everything I was looking at in that room, *I had chosen none of it!* Nothing, nothing, *nothing* I was looking at was there because of some decision I made that it should enter my life and home.

Which was strange to me, because as I thought back to the time I got married, I seemed to recall having stuff! In fact, I was fairly confident that, at the time of my nuptuals, I was the deeded owner of numerous items of personal property. I could still picture many in my mind. But that was the only place I could still picture them, in the dim, cobwebbed corners of my tiny brain, because now all I could see before me was that they had been gradually, systematically and completely replaced by items of Sarah's choosing.

(Sarah, I should explain, is the otherwise bright, witty and beautiful woman whose sole act of unexplained madness was walking down an aisle and reciting marriage vows with me. There can be trouble when someone marries beneath oneself and knows it. Sarah married beneath herself, but she still doesn't know it. And I'm doing my best to keep her in the dark.)

But it didn't stop there. I leapt to my feet, full of purpose. I looked in the kitchen - I'd chosen very little of that. I looked in the bedrooms and bathrooms - I'd chosen very little of that as well. I looked in my own closet - I had chosen *literally* none of that! And ultimately I was rocked yet again, as I realized it was bigger than just the things in my house. Thinking back, I hadn't chosen the house either!

13

So I started to question for the first time whether I was really the captain of this thing I called my life.

I was sitting in a house I hadn't picked out, surrounded by things I hadn't picked out, eating low-fat chips no male would ever pick out, and I thought to ask myself for the first time: How many battles with the women in my life had I won and lost? I thought of the arguments I'd waged with Sarah and other women over the years. I tried to remember my last argument with a woman which ended with her saying, "OK, you're clearly right, you win." Hmmmm . . . . hadn't been that day . . . . week, month or year. Turns out no woman had ever said that to me!

So on that fateful afternoon I had a little ceremony, and I laid my male ego to rest. When you're 40 and it hits you that you've never won an argument with a woman, honestly, what's the point? So I went to the back yard, had a little service, turned over some dirt, shed a tear, said good-bye to my old ego friend, and faced the world for the first time without him. And today, I no longer have a need to be Macho Man. Instead, at my age, I'm content to sit on the couch with a beer and just be Nacho Man.

I began to understand what a wasteful pursuit it is to try to be macho. It dawned on me that only men talk about "saving face." Women seem to know from the start what most men take their whole lives to learn - nobody's really talking about you, so stop dwelling on your "reputation," because it's so very hard to find someone who wants to do it with you. Most women don't waste time with such things. When's the last time you heard a woman talk about "saving face?" That's right - never! Women seem to know that saving face is a black hole you can pour time and energy into and never get anything worthwhile back. If a woman ever does talk about saving face, she means plastic surgery! As in, "The doctor says that for 25 grand, I could save some face."

So I finally put my ego aside and reached the stage in life where I can look myself honestly in the mirror and admit that Everything I Needed To Know I Learned From My Wife.

Now right off the bat, I know not all will agree with me on this. Some fifteen years ago, as you may remember, a man eloquently wrote that "All I Really Need To Know I Learned In Kindergarten." Really?! In kindergarten?? Good for him, God bless him - must be a bachelor. Any man who claims he already learned all he needed to know by the ripe old age of six could not possibly be married. I'm willing to concede that kindergarten may teach you many fine things about sharing and playing nice. But I think one could be an honors graduate of kindergarten, maybe even, I dare say, a Phi Beta Kappa graduate of kindergarten, and still in no way be equipped to deal with the stresses of your wife's pregnancy, childbirth, post-partem depression, PMS, menopause and idiot in-laws.

So I believe the lessons you learn after marriage are the most important. And to all the prospective husbands-in-waiting, let me say that marriage indeed will be the single greatest educational opportunity of your life. Not that you haven't had some education so far. You have, but so far you have been a bachelor, so all you have today is a Bachelor's Degree. Once you're married you're going for your MMA, Masters in Matrimonial Arts. They should say that at the ceremony - "I pronounce you husband and wife. Let the lessons begin!"

And there will be lessons. And this is not a one- or two-semester, not a three- or four-year program. This is lifelong learning, 24/7/365, no Spring or Christmas break. There will be seminars, lectures, punishment, reward and numerous pop quizzes.

The training lasts as long as the marriage lasts, and I would encourage you to look at it this way. If you've been married less than 10 years, you're a freshman. 10 to 20 years, sophomore. 20 to 30 years, junior. And finally, after 30 years, congratulations - you're a senior. Not that you're going to graduate. Even if you've been at it for 80 years, marriage is one school where you're always a couple of credits short.

Rex Havens

Forget everything that medical science has to offer, the compresses and poultices, the laser scalpels and yummy pink medicine. When it comes to mending a strained relationship, nothing holds a candle to the healing power of "I'm sorry."

To many that may seem ridiculously obvious, but men of my generation were blinded to it by a passing cultural phenomenon of our youth. We were blatantly lied to and deceived. I blame the movie "Love Story", over 30 years ago, for misleading an entire generation, because that movie taught us that:

"Love means you never have to say you're sorry."

They even made it into a hit song. Remember?

What? What? What a crock!

Calling all young gentlemen! Do not be fooled. Mayday! Mayday! Pay no attention to that man behind the curtain!

Listen up, young marriageable males:

Love means you never STOP saying you're sorry!

Love means you should start off each day with a big, fat apology before your feet even hit the floor. For whatever you may have done wrong in her dream!

Yes, almost every married man has been scolded and punished *for fun he did not have!*

In fact, young gentelmen, some days that's the reason a husband wakes up. No warning, just a sharp elbow to the ribs, as the love of his life screams, "Do you know what you were doing?" To which he can only reply, "I don't even like your sister!"

"Love Story" should have been banned from the country, or at least given the rarely used FORBA rating - Full Of Really Bad Advice. Or PGW for Pathetically, Grossly Wrong. If subject matter can be banned for indecency, then why not for irresponsibility? How can it be legal to give out mass advice which is tantamount to marital suicide?

Erich Segal, who wrote "Love Story," could not have been more wrong or done a bigger disservice to male/female interaction if he had written "Women like it when you drag 'em by the hair."

Here's what Erich Segal should have written:

Love means, whenever in doubt, say you're sorry. And be constantly in doubt.

Love means say you're sorry for everything you did, said, thought, omitted, inferred, insinuated, suggested, forgot, imagined, deleted or telepathically communicated.

Love means say you're sorry whether or not you know what you're sorry for. The truth is out there, and she will find it.

Love means say you're sorry and sound sincere, because if you're not, she'll know and then you'll really be sorry.

Love means say you're sorry even if you're positive you did nothing wrong and the whole problem is someone else's doing and responsibility. This is a most difficult lesson for a man to learn, because he was taught to say "I'm sorry" only when he regrets something he actually did or caused. But to women, "I'm sorry" is a near-universal cure appropriate in numerous settings, many of which have nothing to do with blaming the one uttering the words.

For example, "I'm sorry" is an appropriate shorthand statement for all of the following:

- "I'm sorry I did that."

- "I'm sorry he/she/it/they did that."

- "I'm sorry you're upset with me."

- "I'm sorry you're upset with anybody."

- "I'm sorry you're upset about anything."

- "I'm sorry Janet wore your same dress to the party."

- "I'm sorry the whole world does not know Janet had a boob job."

- "I'm sorry Janet acts like such an upper-crust snob instead of the poor trash she comes from."

- "I'm sorry Janet didn't die in a fiery propane accident."

In short, a man should learn to say "I'm sorry" any time she's not completely happy. That's really what it means. "I'm sorry" is just short for "I'm sorry you're unhappy about anything in this wide world, sweet love of my life, beat of my heart, glow of my cheeks, spring in my step."

"And, oh yeah, one more thing. That Janet's such a bitch!"

"Man"
The Only Dirty
Three-Letter Word

Surely it's not a good sign for males that the phrase "Oh, Man!" means either that (1) something has gone horribly wrong, or (2) major unpleasantness has occurred.

But that's what we keep saying, every time we miss a bus, burn our tongue, stub a toe, drop our eyeglasses overboard, lose our keys, spill an open paint can, bail a child out of jail, rub a blister, rear-end a squad car, chip a tooth, whiff on the first tee, lose a bet or get an audit notice.

That's not a bad example. Say you've just pulled an IRS invitation from your mailbox. First words? "Oh, Man!" OK, that's the mild version. If you're given to more earthy means of expression, per-haps "Oh, S#&%!" pops out. Which is even more devastating to we males. Because the message there is that when times are bad, "Oh, Man!" and "Oh, S#&%!" mean the same thing! "Man" and "S#&%" - perfectly interchangeable terms! Say one, say the other, say both. It all means the same thing - "How awful!" Man, Oh Man, Oh Man, Oh Man!

And if such language usage gives men a bad self-image, it starts when we're very young, one or two years old. After all, what were we all taught little girls are made of versus what little boys are made of?

What are little girls made of? Oh, yeah, girls are made of "sugar and spice . . . . and everything nice!" Really? Everything nice? Everything nice on the face of the earth was used in the girl-mak-ing process? They used up literally all the nice things making girls!?

How utterly devastating to little boys. "All the nice stuff's gone? Used it all to make girls? Whatya got left over for me?"

"Well, I think we can scrape up some snips and snails and puppy dog tails, how's that sound?"

"Great - load me up! What a relief. I was afraid you'd only have junk left over by now. Whew! Thanks for sparing no expense!"

Really? That's all we men get? Snips and snails and puppy dog tails? Sounds like stuff that wasn't good enough to go into sausage! Slaughterhouse floor scraps, more like. Perhaps that's the order. Little girls first, then sausage, then little boys, waaaaaay at the bottom.

And the word "Man" itself is used so aggressively in speech. "M" - "A" - "N." It's the root word of so many bad words. Like "MAN-slaughter." "MAN-handle." "MAN-hunt." "MAN-o-war." "MAN-ure!"

On a hunch, I conducted a word search to find the most common English phrases containing the words "good man" versus "good woman." The top three "good woman" sayings were all noble and uplifting:

1) "There's nothing you can't do with the love of a good woman."

2) "Behind every successful man, there's a good woman."

3) "I just hope I die in the arms of a good woman."

But on the other hand:

1) "A good man . . . is hard to find!"

2) "Where are all the good men?"

3) "There are no good men!"

23

(Of course, there are a few good men, but the Marines claim to have them all.)

While the world has many good men, no doubt, the idea that men are the more evil of the two genders is advanced at least by inference every day in the media and elsewhere in our lives.

If you watch or read the news, it can seem as though if anything bad happens in the world, 99% of the time, men did it. Which is not to say all men are bad. But since being good is seldom newsworthy, man after man shows up in the news for the evil he does.

If you knew nothing of the general nature of men and women, and you formed your impression solely from the news, you would assume that men are in charge of the crime, lust, greed, corruption, frauds and scams.

On the other hand, women seem to be in charge of more noble pursuits - the loving and the nurturing, the color, the beauty and the texture of life.

Women Good - Men Bad!

Unfair? Certainly. But it's nonetheless that way in the back of most people's minds. Ask yourself when's the last time there was some serial killer on the loose, some unknown, unidentified serial killer running around wreaking mayhem, leaving a trail of fear, and you said to yourself, "Gee, I hope they catch her! How can ya sleep knowing that mad woman's out there? When will these ladies learn?"

But they always catch him, it's always a man, and I always say to myself, "Geez, that was our team! One of ours. We did it again. When will we learn? We should call a meeting."

24

And men keep doing it over and over and over at such a rate it would suggest that we may never learn. There are currently 2.2 million people imprisoned in the United States, and 96% are male. 2.2 million in prison - and over 2 million are men. Men make up 48% of the country's population, but 96% of the prison population. The conclusion is obvious - women are smarter, and don't get caught as often!

It's even more lopsided on death row - 98.5 % men, 1.5% women. It's actually big news when a woman's time is up:

"They're gonna execute another one today."

"So what? What'd this guy do?"

"It's a woman!"

"No way!?

Bonnie and Clyde. Know what made them famous? Here's a hint - it wasn't Clyde! The unique thing about them was that there was a woman at all. Without Bonnie, Clyde would have been just another faceless male bank robber, plenty of 'em to go around, and it's rare they become internationally famous. That's where Clyde was smart - marketing! Because if you can somehow get a woman to help you do anything wicked, you're well on your way to immortality!

Chapter #4

The Red-Eye From Venus Must Have Been A Killer, But Think Of All The Miles You Got!

Rex Havens

Despite the fact that we're wired differently, and the barriers to total understanding may even be insurmountable, both sides keep trying to figure out the other, and we've spawned an impressive pile of theories. Some say our behaviors come from genetics; others say it's all learned. Some say it's basic animal instinct; others say it's environmental. Some trace its roots to prehistoric times; others credit modern phenomena.

A popular '90's theory goes so far as to say it's due to the solar system! Dr. John Gray wrote a book titled "Men Are From Mars, Women Are From Venus", and sold over 24 million copies! 24 million people bought this book! Could there possibly be any greater proof that we will never understand each other than the fact that a man could write a book, the title of which is "Men Are From MARS . . . Women Are From VENUS", and 24 million people would reach for their money, thinking, "That might just be IT!!! Men are from Mars, waaaay over here. And women are from Venus, waaay over there! Sure. Finally, something that makes sense! Here I was limiting myself to single-planet thinking, and all the while the answer was out there in the cosmos. That's it! Ya gotta think outside the globe!"

24 million people so earnestly desperate for answers that they parted with twenty bucks in the hope that maybe, just maybe, they'd understand the opposite sex better by learning more about their planet of origin! These are people who've been muttering to themselves for years that there's no way their partner could have been raised in this world - and along comes John Gray, who says that none of us are truly from here! He says men and women were actually born and raised on completely different planets, then at some age are transported here to this neutral territory, where it's no wonder they have trouble getting along because they're dealing with some of the negative effects of forced intergalactic bussing! They've both been ripped from their natural

environments and forced to coexist with other creatures of vastly different backgrounds. And while they may learn to get along as time goes by, as that old saying goes, you can take the boy out of Mars, but you can't take Mars out of the boy.

Which is not to dismiss the Mars/Venus theory in the least. Maybe there's something to it. Maybe men are from Mars. After all, it's the Red Planet - the angry, surly, vengeful, probably constipated planet - distant, hostile, named after the Roman god of war. Maybe that's why men are such macho buttheads all the time.

And maybe women are from Venus. It's the most beautiful, most mysterious planet - it's the Morning Star, the Evening Star, named after the goddess of beauty and love. It also happens to be the gassy planet. Not that it's wise to bring that up.

One day when Sarah was less than delighted with me, she threatened to write a book, "Women Are From Venus, Men Are A Pain In The Ass!" Then, just in case the first book left any unanswered questions, maybe a sequel, "Men Are From Mars, And They Should Go Back Where They Came From!"

In defense of men, it's important to point out one overlooked fact about the Mars/Venus controversy. Venus is 26 million miles from Earth, so that's how far feminine space-travelers had to come to join the Great Dance. But Mars is 35 million miles from Earth. Which means each man traveled 9 million extra miles for the privilege of getting his name on her dance card. You can fault man's insight, depth, thoughtfulness, understanding, empathy or compassion, but you cannot deny the incontrovertible fact that man put in a 35% greater effort just to be here. Win or lose, men wouldn't have missed this for the world, let alone let a measly 9 million additional miles stand in the way.

26 million miles for woman. 35 million miles for man. 61 million

miles between them. And you thought salmon traveled a long way to mate!

(As an aside, and as a minor item of pride, I would like to point out that this entire discussion of the solar system was completed without a single cheap joke about Uranus. Butt I digress.)

Rex Havens

Even in light of the advances of women in recent generations, some people still maintain that it's a man's world. Though representing a fading minority, it is still an opinion worthy of respect. Most of us come from free countries, where wars were fought so that people might hold different opinions, and we should celebrate that freedom and never forget how special it is. But if anyone really believes it's a man's world, they owe it to themselves to have . . . A WEDDING!

Yes, indeed, young man, on your wedding day, that's when you will find out what an incredibly tiny, tiny piece of that day's puzzle you are.

Many grooms make the same mistake. They go into their wedding day thinking to themselves, "Hey, this is MY wedding day. I'm half of the happy couple. Surely this day is at least somewhat in celebration of . . . ME."

Sorry, fellas. It's not your day. Not your day at all. It's HER day. Not your day.

She doesn't even really want you there!

She'd get married without you if she could. The only reason you even got an invitation is there's a law somewhere that says you've got a right to be notified. She may love you and want to be your wife, but trust me, if she could have that beautiful day and just leave you home on the La-Z-Boy, she'd do it every time. To a woman, a wedding is like a ham sandwich - if you're going to have one, unfortunately, somebody's got to invite the pig!

No matter how much she loves you, you're still a man, which means that, on the wedding day, in her mind, you're an accident waiting to happen. You've gotta be watched, coached, monitored, rehearsed, spoon-fed, baby-sat and kept on schedule. You will not be trusted with a single major decision about the day - flowers, colors, fabrics, decorations, nothing. She'd like to let you, but frankly, you're too stupid.

You probably won't even be allowed to pick out the clothing you'll wear that day. Perhaps you've been dressing yourself and making your own sartorial decisions for 20 or 30 years by now. But not today. You're just too stupid.

Only she possesses the right sense of composition and proportion to make all the complex design decisions required to make it the perfect presentation, the perfect day.

And let me say I agree completely with letting her make these decisions. I fully believe that the average woman has a much better sense of the artistic and the aesthetic than the average man. When I got married, I found out my darling Sarah wanted checks for the checkbook that were . . . get this . . . pretty! I'm a man; I just wanted checks that would clear! The way I see it, if I write a check and the bank pays it, that is one beautiful document. Did just what it was supposed to do. No pain, no penalty, no "NSF" stamped on it - mission accomplished! The full range of financial beauty as I know it. Whether it looks like a sunrise or a baboon's backside, makes no difference; both are equally beautiful.

Sarah also informed me we were going to divide the checkbook. I got the deposit slips.

So I say, men, on the wedding day, let her make the decisions, and gladly. It's her day, not your day. It's the way it's always been and the way it always will be. This author makes no attempt to change things here, men, and neither should you. It could only end badly. Accept your limited role, and know it going in. Things will go better for you.

Everything is about her, as it should be. It starts with the engagement photo in the paper. Who's in the photo? In some papers, they both are, but in others, it's just one. When it's just one, which one? Yes, the bride. Hey, if you're only going to show one, isn't it just common sense it should be the *important* one?

Next, her gown. The search for it may take weeks, even months. It will cost hundreds, often thousands of dollars. There will be five separate fittings, it must fit perfectly. After the ceremony, her dress will be carefully, lovingly cleaned, pressed, folded, sealed, wrapped in plastic, saved, preserved, treasured and revered as an altar and shrine for life.

His clothing is . . . rented.

And must be back to the shop on Monday.

Because another guy needs it next weekend!

A minor difference, fellas. Hardly worth mentioning. Don't let it bother you that five hundred other men got married in your suit. Five hundred. That's how many rentals before a tux is so tattered they cannot in good conscience rent it to one more guy. Five hundred wearings! But you're still special.

Fifty years from now the bride can hold up her gown and say, "I got married in that." If the groom can do that, he'll be holding underwear!

Rex Havens

Wedding rings.

The bride's ring stops traffic. Everyone wants to see it, gasp at it, talk about it, know all the details of size and cut and the story of how he gave it to her.

And this ring is incredible. You're supposed to spend three month's income on her ring. Know who says so? The American Diamond Association! What a shock.

Now I spent three months income on Sarah's ring, and she was still mad. I chose June, July and August from the summer I turned thirteen. It was my money, so I thought I got to pick the time frame. I figured I had a loophole. Apparently not.

Her ring is amazing, a thing of sculpted, precise beauty. Thousands of dollars.

His ring? $82.50. Most stores throw it in when you buy hers.

It's the jeweler's way of saying, "Hey, fella, we ripped you off on that rock pretty bad. Whatya say this piece of junk's on the house. No, please, take it. Here, take six or seven, we got 'em in a bucket back here. Take a fistful, go ahead. Wear one on your foot if you like. Really. They don't cost us nuthin'. We use 'em for packing peanuts. You deserve it. You're a good boy."

Diamonds are a girl's best friend.

Man's best friend . . . . is a dog.

Who thought that up? _Women_ thought that up!

Who else could have come up with that? Woman's best friend is one of the most beautiful, precious, rarest things on the planet. Man's best friend is so plentiful we neuter them because we don't want more!

It's very hard to get woman's best friend - it's three miles down in an African diamond mine. Where do we get man's best friend? "My neighbor had an extra, he gave it to me. He was just gonna shoot it, so I took it off his hands. Price was right. He's my buddy."

Gentlemen, we must face facts. They beat us on this one. Women have a best friend over which nations have waged wars and for which airtight security must be vigilantly maintained. Man's best friend leaves behind "presents" nobody is happy to receive. "Presents" left around so carelessly and abundantly we actually step in them. "Oh, Man!"

But now let's risk making the women angry. Because it's time to reveal a secret about their "best friend" which women have managed to keep under wraps for centuries, and which they'd probably like to keep buried indefinitely. Ready? Diamonds are not actually rare! In fact, by all evidence, far from it. Diamonds are apparently quite abundant, and probably not worth anywhere near what men have been convinced to pay for them.

Don't believe me? Think I should be tortured with a thousand sharp ends from a thousand Cartier ear studs? Then consider this: If something is rare, shouldn't there occasionally be shortages?

It's perhaps the most basic rule of the marketplace. If something is truly rare, there will be times when you can't get it, find it or buy it, not at any price. In fact, that's what "rare" means -- "not always obtainable."

But ask yourself, in your entire life, have you ever walked into a jewelry store and been told, "Sorry, we're out."? Have you ever left the house intent on a diamond purchase, only to come home empty-handed, with the explanation that, "Unfortunately, even though the miners are working triple shifts, they just haven't found any this month."?

Not me. In fact, I've never been to a big mall that didn't have at least six jewelry stores, with not a single empty display case, not even a single empty slot in a case to be found among the whole lot of them. Every display unit full, more in the back, more coming tomorrow, more next week, don't worry, if you want it, it's here, and it's yours. If diamonds were any less scarce, the mall would be nothing but jewelry stores, with Foot Locker and The Gap evicted as homeless orphans forced to operate out of the trunk of a Chevy.

In contrast, I have seen merchants run out - dead out! - of strawberries, melons, grapefruit, canola oil, coffee, eggs, bread, sugar and syrup. Impending natural disasters cause runs on cereal and Fruit Roll-Ups. International trade snags foster the occasional paper shortage. I've lived through times when I couldn't buy gasoline. Heck, in the middle of January I've even seen stores be out of rock salt and snow shovels! But I've never seen jewelers be even so much as low on diamonds, a commodity so hopelessly rare it's always available.

Come to think of it, we've heard predictions for the last 30-40 years that the world has only enough oil for another 30-40 years. Ever heard a forecast on how many more years before we harvest the last diamond? It has to be out there, doesn't it? The world's last diamond, waiting to be unearthed? Could it be our generation should quit buying them so there'll be some left for our grandchildren? I suggested that to Sarah. Know what she said? "Oh, Man!"

So now, my young groom friend, your wedding day has arrived. You've put a rock that cost more than your first two cars on her hand, she's picked out your tux, and the magic day is here. Try your best to stop throwing up, it's going to be great. And, oh yes, to repeat, only because it's so important it bears repeating, you're both getting married, but you're doing in on *HER* day.

Your first clue was well before the wedding, because you may have noticed that once you're engaged, you have to "register." This surprises most men. "Register? You mean like a handgun?" No, no, not with the state, with the stores! You "register" for the gifts you want people to buy. And by "you" we mean "her," because all grooms find out that the happy couple only registers for *feminine* things! You register for china, linen, silver and crystal. You never register at the liquor store, the gun shop or the pool hall. There are never any Hooter's gift certificates in those packages, no matter how thoughtful, generous and appreciated that might be.

Her day. She gets her own carpet for the ceremony. I envy that. What a nice touch! They wait until the last moment when she's about to come out, then - whoosh! - they unroll her own special carpet. The carpet's not for the groom. He only gets to walk on it if he goes through with the ceremony, then only on the way out, and only by her side. Other than that, fella, stay off the rug. Pretty good rule for the rest of the marriage, too. Stay off the rug, big guy. It can only turn out badly.

Her day. She gets a veil. What a note of elegance! After all, her face is the central visual gift of the day, and her loveliness will eventually be shared and admired by the beloved guests. But first, to maintain suspense, her face is delicately veiled, so that she may glide down the aisle in stately mystery, arrive at the altar, where she is dramatically unveiled, and everyone gasps at her beauty.

The groom's face . . . is at the end of his neck, just like always. No special day for his face. Sorry, pal.

Her day. Her entrance into the church is magical. Everyone stands, everyone turns, there is special music, all because the bride is almost here. And even then, the anticipation must build as she first sends in the bridesmaids. Someone in the crowd (always a man) gets confused when the first woman he sees is not the bride. "Honey, that's not Susan. I know that's not her. Are we in the right church? . . . What? Oh, I get it, sample women first. Bride appetizers. OK, I'm with the program now. Bring 'em on down."

And each bridesmaid is doing that time-honored, halting, stag-gered, one-baby-step-at-a-time Wedding Walk. You know the one. Like your dog right after he got fixed.

That's her entrance, and it's truly grand, breathtaking, sentimental and timelessly memorable. And the groom's entrance? A little less. The clergyman explains it to him at rehearsal. "OK, Jim, now tomorrow we'd like you to come in through the alley door over here. Just come in quiet-like at no particular time when nobody gives a rip, that's how we do it here. Don't attract atten-tion to yourself. Just drag your little puppy-dog-tail self to the center here, and if you do it right, the whole crowd'll look up and go, 'Where the heck did he come from? Doesn't he at least get a bell or a whistle?'"

Oh, yes, my young grooms, on the biggest day of a man's life, he'll be standing in an alley next to a dumpster with hungry cats at his feet. His friends are handing him the keys to a Nissan so old it's a Datsun.

(Because that's the rule in most marriages - it's the man's job to drive the bad car. It's true in over 90% of marriages. She drives the new, comfy car - he drives the sputtering death trap with no air conditioning or radio. He drives to work singing the Husband Song. "Yeah, I'm a married man, married man, married man. I got a ring and a thermos and a rusty car, I'm a married man, married man, married man." In the parking lot at work, he waves to guys in other rusty cars. "Hey, Bill, ya got 400,000 miles on that thing yet? Gee, Tony, is that new? Wow! Nice thermos! How can he afford that? I bet he's makin' payments.")

Remember this, fellas, and it puts it all in perspective. There's a "special song" for her entrance, and it is in fact popularly called "Here Comes The Bride." Red alert - there is no special music for your entrance. Nothing. Never been even one written, not in all the history of music. And by now you'd think there would be a song about literally everything. Millions of composers writing for millions of years.

There are songs about trains, shipwrecks, Chevrolets, GTO's, little Nash Ramblers, little deuce coupes, bubble gum, suede shoes, Love Potion #9, lollipops, doing it my way, doing the twist, doing the monster mash, doing drugs, doing time and doing it in the road. Songs about fame, fortune, the grapevine, don't sleep in the subway, that voodoo that you do, streakers, roller derby and Doo-Wah-Ditty-Ditty-Dum-Ditty-Do!

Songs about Georgia, San Jose, San Francisco, New York, Chicago, Houston, Kokomo, Paris, London, Tokyo, Shanghai, Santa Catalina, singin' in the rain and walkin' in Memphis.

Not to mention songs about dying, crying, lying, flying, buying, spying, prying, trying and sighing. Tributes to rock & roll, rock-a-billy, rocket man, jailhouse rock, rocky top, rock around the clock, love you like a rock, big rock candy mountain and the big bad rock of ages. The magic touch, magic man, black magic woman, this magic moment, do you believe in magic and Puff the Magic Dragon.

Odes to Dolly, Rhonda, Layla, Sharona, King Tut, Sloopy, Mame, Barbara Ann, Bill I love you still, a boy named Sue, and girls with nothing more going for them than junk in the trunk.

All Renee had to do was walk away and she got a song. Some girl from Ipanema got a song, and nobody even knows her name. Not that lack of a name makes her unique, because there are songs about a brown-eyed girl, a devil in a blue dress, a "pretty woman" and girls who just wanna have fu-un. Heck, some horse with no name got both a song and the title! And some no-name guy got a song for doing nothing more than to just drop in to see what condition his condition was in.

So you'd think everybody would have a song by now, and not merely the just and virtuous. Even Leroy Brown has a song, and he's bad. Bad. Bad to the bone.

But turn over every last page of sheet music ever written and you'll not find a single tune devoted to the fact that a groom is about to walk to the altar. Lay, lady lay across my big brass bed, but nary a note for a man to be wed!

And there probably never will be. Because what could they call it?

"Show Up, Shut Up & Smile"?

Chapter #8

She's The Focus. Get The Picture?

Her day. And I want to say, from the heart, that if I could press a button and be a woman for a year, I'd do it at the drop of a hat. Because I would love to understand the depth of friendships that women have for each other. I believe it's deeper than any two men have ever known.

Gentlemen, have you ever seen what it's like when one woman asks another to be in her wedding? This is simply the greatest excitement any two people on this earth can share. Light years beyond any two men at any Super Bowl celebration ever. If you've witnessed it, you know it is beyond description. There is just nothing like the moment . . . when one woman . . . looks deep into the eyes . . . of her good friend . . . . . . eyes wide as basketballs . . . . arms flailing . . . . gasping for breath . . . as she lovingly squeaks: " . . . Wait, wait, wait . . . . . Are you ready for this? . . . . . wait, wait . . . . I don't believe it . . . . . wait . . . . . . sit down, sit down . . . . I want . . . I want . . . . *I want you to be in the wedding!*"

And the friend . . . . lovingly and on cue . . . . wets herself.

"OOOOOOOOOOOOHH! I'm so HAPPY for you!!! This is toooo wonderful! I LOVE you so much! Geeeez, there's so much to do! Oooh, oooh, what are your colors, WHAT ARE YOUR COLORS??!!"

Who in their right mind wouldn't want to be in on that? Anybody not enjoy celebrating? Surely not. Celebration, by definition is fun. And everybody loves fun, because it's so much fun!

And what a tremendous celebration it is! The running and jumping and kissing and hugging, for the honor - no, the privilege - of spending $500 on the ugliest dress you've ever seen in your life. After three or four bridal showers, this wedding will easily cost each bridesmaid a grand. But they don't care. They're honored, and happy, because they truly love their friend that much.

It's not the same for the groom. He walks into work on Monday: "Hey, Tom . . . . aw, man, I hate to do this. But . . . I got . . . I got seven spots to fill. Nah, they had a meeting, that's all I know, and it's seven. Got word over the weekend, it's in stone, no changing it. And, look, I know we haven't hung around for a few years, but I've always thought of you as my seventh best friend. So, what I'm sayin' is . . . . I need you to stand up with me."

His friend's reaction? "Oh, man, that's SIXTY BUCKS! Oh, man! Isn't there anybody else you can nail this one on? You got a paperboy, don't you, or a cousin . . . . somebody from grade school? How 'bout that guy in the park, 'Will work for food'? Oh, cripes! There'd better be an open bar, that's all I'm sayin'. I see a cash bar, I'm walkin'. Open bar, at least I can break even. Oh, I can drink back a tux rental, done 'er before."

Her day. The clergyman asks, "Who gives this woman to be married to this man?" Again, she's protected and elevated as a precious asset. Her family gets to decide if she goes or stays.

Her father, having just handed the bride off at the altar, now sits there conferring with her mother, asking, "Honey, whadya think? Should we keep her . . . or give her to dipstick over there? You think he's all right? Never liked him myself, what about you? I think there's a time limit, sweetheart, reverend seems to want an answer. Ah, well . . . OK . . . her mother and I do."

The groom's family, on the other hand, is not consulted at all. It is presumed they are delighted anyone wants him in the first place. His family's over there saying, "Yeah, let her wash his dirty shorts for a while. We'll see how love blooms in that fertilizer."

And there the new couple stands, before a person of the cloth, who "pronounces" them husband and wife. That's right, you get "pronounced" husband and wife. One of only two times in this world you get "pronounced" something.

Married . . . . and dead.

It may not sound comforting, but it is what we say. Some people get "pronounced" married, and, unfortunately, others get "pronounced" dead. But it makes sense, because they're very similar experiences. For either way, people pray, people cry, and they haul you off in a nice car.

So that's it. Now you're "Man and Wife. "Mr. and Mrs." Mister - "M-R" - two letters. Missus - "M-R-S" - three letters. Gentlemen, her title is 50% bigger than yours. Shouldn't that have been a clue?

You're man and wife now. Time to break in some new vocabulary. Marriage has its own terminology, and the groom has to get up to speed, and quickly.

For example, Mr. Newlywed, your new wife will henceforth be referred to as your "better half." As in, "Boss, I'd like you to meet Nancy, my better half." "Better half." You're part of a team now, fella, a team with two halves. This team has a better half - and she's it! But by definition that means the team necessarily has a lesser, embarrassing, inferior half - and welcome to the party, son!

Man and wife. My schooling started immediately, right at the reception. I hadn't been married more than an hour before I was staring into the face of Lesson One.

Everyone wanted to take photos. Sarah, my new wife, the Blushing Bride, was in all of them. Sarah was in constant demand. No camera flash lit up without her smiling face center stage in front of it.

I, on the other hand, was in . . . some of them. We had been wed, had become one, but it turned out we were really more like 1-A and 1-B. Every shot started with Sarah, and built from there.

I only entered the frame after someone said something like, "Oh, why don't you get in there, too?"

Lesson Two followed immediately at the punch bowl. The hostess handed Sarah two cups of punch, but as Sarah turned to me, she looked disdainfully down into one of them and said, "Oh, darn it, this one's got a fly in it." And without a moment's moral hesitation, she extended an arm and gave me the bad one. Her innate, bridely reaction: "Oooh! Contaminated! Icky! Yours!" My reaction was equally innate. I accepted it, fished out the offending floater, and drank it. I was a husband now: "Oooh! Contaminated! Icky! Yummmm!"

Chapter 9

"Women And Children First!"
Got A Problem With That?

I noted earlier the comparison between diamonds as a girl's best friend, while man's is a dog, and I advanced the theory that women came up with this idea. Yes, I believe women thought it up, fellas, and here's how. Ready?

Because they're smarter than us!

That's right, I'm truly sorry, and I hope each man finds the strength to go on. But drop that male ego out of gear for just a minute, look at it rationally, and there's little escaping it. Not every battle, not on every front. We men win a few here and there. But many times, on many subjects, they're smarter, they've beaten us, and we might do well to learn a lesson and profit from it rather than continuing to deny the situation.

Not that women usually flaunt it. They don't waste a lot of time bragging. Some women even believe that part of being smarter is pretending not to be smarter - unlike most men, who have to be stroked and praised and reassured all the time. "Oh, you're the greatest. What would we do without you???" In contrast, it's enough for most women to rule quietly, secure in the knowledge that it's mostly their agenda being followed, their orchestra, play-ing their melody. You don't have to tell most women they're in charge. They know they're running the place, and they know it in a calm, quiet, secure, confident way.

So I say women thought up the diamond/dog best friend thing because that time they were smarter than men, no contest. Here's one I guarantee women thought up: "Women and children first!" To which man can only stand by and say, "Uh, . . . OK. No, I'm glad you said something, honey, I was about to crawl into the lifeboat. D'you believe that? Forgot my assignment, stay here and die!! No, you go ahead sweetheart, you're the precious cargo. We'll be all right, no we won't, but you go on. Us guys are gonna go to the back of the ship, lock arms and sing 'Kum-Ba-Ya.' See what it's like to be a shark-sicle!"

Anybody think that was a man's idea? Couldn't be. Women thought it up, convinced men it was noble, and today we accept it without question. Had it been up to me, if the world had some-how asked me what I thought the rule should be, I would have said "Children first" - sure, let them have their future. After that, I say we go by upper body strength. If you can kick my tail, you've earned a seat in the boat. But at least work for it and earn it. This is America, right?

But, no, it'll never change, it's too deeply ingrained. It'll always be "Women and children first," and only after that does a different rule kick in - "Every man for himself!" Things sure turn primitive once the women and kids are gone.

Think about that. "Women and children first." We learn it so early, practically from birth. It's presumed to be such a basic rule, one we never question, a central part of life itself. And it's not the only one. Women have a better public relations machine working for them than men could ever dream of or pay for.

There are lots of very feminine-friendly phrases that we learn quite young and accept throughout our lives as basic truths:

"It's a woman's prerogative to change her mind."

You have to stand in awe, men! Because that one is simply GENIUS! It's her *prerogative* to change her mind! So if a woman says one thing, but does another, shut up, what's wrong with you, she's entitled, that's her privilege! Of course, if a man does the same thing, he's an a- . . . . . he's a . . . . . well, let's just say it starts with "a" and ends with "sshole", that's what he is.

"Hell hath no fury like a woman scorned."

Very poetic, intellectual, lyrical, educated way of saying if you get on the wrong side of a woman, you're actually going to wish you were in hell. Hell would be Club Med compared to where you're going to be.

"A woman's work is never done."

Usually because one of her ongoing projects is a man!

You're married now, fella, and only some of what used to pass for English in your life is going to carry over. The married man has to get used to saying, hearing and interpreting many new phrases he seldom, if ever, had to deal with before he stood at the front of a church and, like Columbus, crossed over into the great unknown. Here they are, and like Kevin Costner said in "Bull Durham," get to know them, they are your friends.

When a young man is about to get married, he imagines that the words he will hear most often are "I love you." They're not. You know what's number one?

"I'll just have some of yours!"

> *Husband:* "Honey, I'm gonna get some more barbecue. You want some?"
>
> *Wife:* "I'll just have some of yours."
>
> *Husband:* "I was gonna get more lemonade. You?"
>
> *Wife:* "Mmmmm . . . I'll just have some of yours."
>
> *Husband:* (under his breath) "The hell you will. I'll bring you your own plate with your own food on it, but this stuff on this plate is mine!"

Men, here's a little tip. When I get a good bratwurst - and I love a good brat - I instantly load it up with mustard and hot sauce. I don't even personally like mustard and hot sauce, but it keeps Sarah away from it. I call it "Wife Repellent" at my house, and it happens to work. You learn to like it for the privacy.

Sarah has ten words which scare me to death:

"But we were in luck, 'cuz it was on sale."

If finding a sale is the standard by which luck is measured, then I have been very, very lucky in my life. I may be one of the luckiest men alive. Recently Sarah bought a $1200 piece of jewelry, BUT we were in luck, 'cuz it was on sale, and she got it for $600. Which means in her mind, she spent $600, but she saved $600, therefore it was free!

And now we have a second problem. Remember that $600 she saved? What are we gonna spend that on? Life gets complicated when you're as lucky as we are!

There are five words every new husband should look out for because, if your wife says them, she's lying! It doesn't matter that she's the sweetest creature ever to stand in the sunlight, that you're sure she's never told you a lie, and you don't even think she's capable. If she says these five words, do not believe her. Ready? Here they are:

"I . . . JUST . . . HOPE . . . YOU'RE . . . HAPPY!"

Do not - repeat - do NOT be fooled! It would be such a mistake to just walk away blissfully thinking, "Great, she's just glad I'm happy." Because those words are Wife Code for "Eat dirt and die!"

Same thing if she says "fine." If you say, "Honey, I'm gonna play cards with the boys tonight" and she says, "Great, have a good time," do you know what that means? It means "Great, have a good time." But if you say "I'm gonna play cards with the boys" and she says "Fine!"? Do not - repeat - do NOT be fooled! Because it means "Eat dirt and die," too!

And it's important men know that these red flags mean trouble, because many women won't come right out and tell the men in their lives that they're "mad." For some reason, many women dislike the word "mad" and will never confess to being "mad." Sarah hates to admit she's "mad" as much as the average man hates to admit he's lost. Sarah's never "mad." She will, however, enlighten me on the appropriate terminology.

I'm a simple beast, so I'll use simple language and ask, "Why are you mad?"

Comes the hair-splitting reply: "I'm not mad. I'm disappointed. Miffed, aggravated, hurt. Wounded, peeved, annoyed, irked, upset, frustrated, irritated, depressed, anxious, edgy, nervous, tense, bothered, infuriated, angry, incensed, concerned, perturbed, uneasy, troubled, worried, sad, exasperated, apprehensive, discontent, dismayed, disturbed, distressed, displeased, distraught, disconcerted, disillusioned, disgruntled, disgusted, despondent, dejected, let down, unhappy and a little blue ... but I am not MAD!"

"That's good news, honey, I was worried we had a problem there for a second."

Here's another phrase every new husband should get used to saying:

"So, are you gonna tell me what's wrong or not?"

And you know the answer, fellas? No! She's not going to tell you. Why? Because if you loved her, you'd know!!!

There are so many new words to learn because now you're married. You might say that's nothing to be afraid of. They're just words, and after all, we live in the land of free speech. Well . . .

not entirely free. Not when you're married. I put the pencil to it, and I calculated that over the course of my marriage, every time Sarah starts a conversation, on average, it costs about 80 bucks. Sometimes more, sometimes less, but at the end of the year, when I totaled it up, it's an average of about $80 every time that sweet love of my life starts talking.

That doesn't mean men need to be afraid of every conversation. Some conversations are free. Like when Sarah says, "Good morn-ing! It's a nice day. Did you sleep well?" No cost at all. However, beware of any conversation which begins with the words,

"I've been thinking."

There's about a kazillion different ways to end that sentence. "I've been thinkin' about the house . . . the yard . . . the patio . . . our vacation . . ." - whatever! If Sarah's been thinkin', it's usually at least a grand. And it often comes with a loan application and monthly payments. Men sometimes get the bum rap that we're uncommunicative. Let's set the record straight. Men have noth-ing against communication. It's just that some weeks, we're tapped out. "Sorry, honey, payday's Friday, can we talk then?"

And while we're on the subject of language, I should point out that men might not be so commitment-phobic if the terminology weren't so terrifying to the male mind. A simple look at the words we use to describe marriage is enough to send most men running for the nearest monastery:

"WEDLOCK" - Sounds like prison. If you want men to look forward to being "wed", you should not team it up with "lock", which, let's face it, is not a warm and fuzzy word. No one's ever happy about being locked up, locked down, locked in or locked out. So it should come as no surprise that men are pretty nervous about jumping into "wedlock." You can practically hear the cell door slam! CLANK! "This is the warden speaking, welcome to WEDLOCK. We only have a few rules here at the Big House and they all end with "call home first." Wanna have a drink with the boys? Call home first. Makin' weekend plans? Call home first. And if you're even thinkin' about writing a check for over twenty bucks, we hope you know the drill by now, call home first."

"BALL & CHAIN" - Definitely prison! With the added bonus of rusty leg irons, ponderous weight, the clanking of chains and the dread of sharing a cell with the Count of Monte Cristo.

"TIE THE KNOT" - What they do in prison to the rope before they hang you. How comforting!

So, women, if you want men to change their attitudes toward marriage, start by changing the language. Use words more friendly to the male psyche, terms that will make him want to race headlong to the altar.

How about . . . "Eroto-mania?" No? "Euphoriation?" Wait . . . this is it . . . "Orgasmolympics!" Yes! Trust me, the "Orgasmolympics" would not only cure commitment-phobia, but men would be clawing over each other to make the team.

"Did you hear about Jimmy?"

"No, what?"

"He made it. She said yes, and he's going to the Orgasmolympics. Swears he's gonna bring home a medal."

"Jimmy? Wow. Lucky stiff. Next year, I'm makin' the squad. Nothing can stop me!"

Chapter 11

Seven Things Husbands Should Learn To Say

Alas, we poor, dull males are mired in a communication mindset which sabotages any hope we might have to be on the same frequency as our wives. Because men believe that after we've said something once - one time - then it's out there, as good as in stone, past our own lips, from our own mouths, on the record, established, for all to know, and permanently embedded in the minds of all who heard it. Those were our male words, we said them, we meant them, we stand by them. End of story.

But odds are, fellas, your wife doesn't work that way. And she wishes you didn't either.

Let's say she comes home after a marathon session at the beauty shop. New hairdo, color change, possibly a skin treatment to restore that youthful "glow." She has a happy, expectant look on her face when she walks in the house. And you're a considerate guy, you know where she went, you can see she's waiting for some word from you, and you respond. "You look great, honey. I love what they did!"

And you're proud of yourself. That was an opportunity to succeed or fail, and you soared. Another man might have dropped the ball, but not you. You said the right thing at the right moment with the right tone. Victory. You contemplate rewarding yourself with a beer, even though it's only 11 AM.

You consider it a job well done, and therein lies your mistake. The job is not done, only begun. What many men fail to realize is that the compliment you gave her so convincingly at 11 AM has a shelf-life of no more than 90 minutes!

This news is shocking to a man, I know. It is literally inconceivable to the male mind. But gentlemen, by 12:30, it will be as though you never said a thing. Those praiseful, thoughtful words you were so proud of are on their last legs, and will expire, unless renewed. The stone tablet you thought you had inscribed them on is rapidly crumbling to sand, and you must take up your chisel again, and pronto!

Find a way, and do it. Say to one of the kids at lunch, "Doesn't your Mom look great?" Wasn't that easy? Five little words. One quick breath. And you just bought yourself another 90 minutes!

But 2 PM's approaching. As she walks by, suddenly blurt out, "When's the salon gonna take back this young schoolgirl and bring back my wife?" Now you're golden till 3:30. Nice going! Hey, now's not too early for a beer, is it?

Keep this up for the first day, at least. Whether treatment needs to continue into a second day or beyond will vary, so be alert and don't let your guard down until you're sure it's safe. Then have two beers, no matter what time it is.

Women, try to remember that the reason it's so hard to get men to understand this concept of the continuing compliment is that not only are men trained to believe that once something's been said there's no need to say it again, but men are also conditioned to believe that if words do have to be repeated, there may be severe consequences. Many of our fathers brought us to laser-beam attention with the warning, "I'm not going to tell you again!" Followed shortly by a beating, which was an earlier and more physical version of time-out.

Among male friends, saying something once is always enough. If a guy tells his friend, "You're the best stickball player on the block," that friend will never forget those words, or let the one who said them forget it. Ever! They might even make it onto his headstone.

Repeatedly compliment a man about the same thing every few hours, and he'll get tired of hearing it, sometimes to the point of being physically uncomfortable! "Enough already. Change the subject. Thanks, but let's talk about something else."

That's because compliments between men never expire! If a man says it, he means it, and he means it for all time. Remember, it's only a woman's prerogative to change her mind. (Chapter 9) Men, on the other hand, are stuck with their pronouncements, both the wise and the foolish. But only for eternity.

So men should know that encouraging words for the women in their lives need to be repeated periodically, or they lose their potency. With that in mind, I went in search of the most impor- tant statements and phrases useful to the modern husband. I was after the key sentences a good man should learn to say to a good woman if he wants to keep her for a good long time. It was a long and grueling search, but after years of patient and some- times painful observation, I compiled seven items of wisdom - many difficult for men to say - which kept rising above the others. Gentlemen, this may be bitter medicine, but it's important, so here they are:

1.   **"You were right - I was wrong."**

2.   **"I'm sorry and that won't happen again."**

3.   **"How could I be so stupid?"**

4.   **"I don't deserve you, sweetheart."**

5.   **"I would marry you all over again."**

6.   **"No, you're much prettier than she is."**

7.   "No, if anything that dress makes your butt look _too small!_ "

And, as an expansion of #7, if necessary: "Really, honey, you should eat something, you're just about to blow away. I don't even know how your slacks stay on your hips. There just isn't any meat for 'em to grab onto!"

I learned #7 the hard way.

Now make no mistake - I love Sarah to death. She will always be the best thing that ever happend to me, I have no idea why such a fine woman would stick around and I shall keep her as long as she is misguided enough to stay.

But one day I came home and Sarah ambushed me with a question. I didn't have time to . . . whatya call that? . . . think? She said, "Will you still love me when I'm fat & sassy?" And I said, "You're not thinkin' about turnin' sassy on me, are you?"

In the world of trial and error, that was an error. Huge error!

In fact, gentlemen, allow me to advise that when you are tempted to make a snappy comeback like that to something she says, you are being faced with what I call a split-second "Wife-or-Death" decision.

You can understand a lot about our differences by the way each gender reacts to that joke the many times I have told it. The general male reaction to "You're not thinking about turning sassy on me?" is one of respect, approval and applause. "Oh, that's a good one! Clever, well done! You fought valiantly, brave knight!"

But women boo - and loudly! Even more, I have had popcorn, napkins, pretzels, pizza and ice hurled at me over the years by women who are, in essence, saying, "You are a dead man!" And I completely love that about women. They care about Sarah, even though they've never met her. But they sense one of their own has been wounded! And that's enough. So they circle the wagons, and they say with one voice, "We're gonna get him!"

Women, be proud, be very proud of that instinct. It elevates you. A man seldom cares about another man he's never met. A man will laugh hysterically at his own best friend, caught in some humiliating situation - perhaps just having walked through a plate glass window (lots of mess and at least some blood, yes, that's a good one) - twisting in the wind. A man will laugh and point and call over others to share in his best friend's misery. "Oh, man, you are an idiot! Fellas, come look at this fool over here. You guys ever see such a loser? We're having T-shirts made! You are the moron of the century, my friend. I love ya buddy, but you had yer head way up yer keester. Wait! That's what we'll print on the T-shirts. 'Bill really had his head in his glass on that one!'"

So to all the women over the years who have run to Sarah's defense when I've told the "fat & sassy" joke, let me commend you for your heart and compassion, but let me also assure you that Sarah does not need your protection. She's a very strong woman, and can and does take very good care of herself. She still tells everyone that, years ago, the instant she agreed to marry me, she looked down and saw that her hands were suddenly all skinned up and rough. Because that's what happens when you scrape the bottom of the barrel!

Chapter 12

Mall Mission Impossible:
The Depth And Intricacy Of The Female Mind
(Fellas, We're In Over Our Heads!)

Rex Havens

Gentlemen, remember the gentle suggestion that "They're smarter than us" from a while back? Well, if you cannot help but fight the idea, you'll likely surrender once you've spent any considerable time in the company of a woman at the mall. Shopping has to hold the ultimate proof of the superiority of the female mind. What is that proof? It's the truly staggering list of products and choices which women mentally catalog and process every day, compared to the paltry few men encounter. I truly believe the average woman has to make more decisions before eight in the morning than the average man has to make all day.

But, to new husbands, let me explain that before these great secrets are revealed, you must first learn the ritual of hitting the mall together, which means you must master the Shopping Dance, which differs from all other dances you've previously learned in one major regard - the woman leads! Yes, the Shopping Dance is a formation performed with the woman in front, and her husband a respectful few feet behind and several degrees to one side, and from there it's simple: JUST FOLLOW HER AROUND! Don't lose sight of her, don't let the gap between you grow too wide, and try not to rear-end her when she stops. And as you perform your supporting role in this serpentine Shopping Dance, as she winds her way through a maze of racks and bins, you must continue to repeat the following mantra: "No, I'm right here, honey. Right behind you. I got your flank. I'm your wingman, sweetheart. Blue Light Leader, you are free to browse, free to browse, there are no bogies in sight. Repeat, this is a target-rich environment, show no mercy, charge at will and take no prisoners!"

Once you have mastered the Shopping Dance, men, next open your eyes to the truly awesome vastness and intricacy of the world these women command. I hope it's true that men and women are equally intelligent - all available physical and neurological studies say they are. But, gentlemen, women must be using more of their brains than we are, because they keep track of so much more information than we do.

Case in point - shoes. On the surface, it sounds simple. After all, how complicated can basic footwear be? And men's shoes, it's true, are simple and basic. In fact, they're called simply "shoes." Just "shoes." Regardless of style, if it goes at the end of a man's leg, it has but one name - it's a "shoe."

Women, on the other hand, don't have a single pair of anything generically known as "shoes." They have subcategories and sub-species for every change in footwear. Women have pumps . . . and clogs . . . and flats and slings . . . and heels and open-toed and mules and spikes . . . and flip-flops and strappy sandals and scrunchy boots . . . stilettos and wedges! Men don't know what any of these are. It's a code they use to keep us out of the con-versation. A man doesn't know a pump from a flat. All a man knows is, "When ya got a flat, you need a pump!"

And the colors that women memorize! How is it that women know every name for every color ever invented? It's an endless list, but for women, apparently it is no big problem. Every woman in the world knows, for example, what color "periwinkle" is!

There aren't one hundred men in the universe who can identify periwinkle. Because men only know the eight colors in the big fat crayon box from first grade. In fact, we've forgotten about six of those; most of us are pretty well down to black and brown that we can confidently recognize.

But women know every color, tint, shade, pastel, variation and gradation of hue. Sarah's shoe catalog - what a mind-boggling collection of complexity! Exotic names I had never seen before. Aspen, mauve, ecru, taupe. Seabreeze, eggshell, crimson, indigo. Khaki, beige, honeysuckle, ivory, lavender, sandstone, heather, mist, teal, satin, flax, coral, cream, nugget, pearl, saddle, daisy, black, ebony, charcoal, raven, midnight, parsley, persimmon, pineapple, periwinkle, papaya, peach, purple, pink, poppy, pixie, powder, pewter, peapod, pansy, pumpkin, puce, pomegranate, peppermint, pancake, pumpernickel, champagne . . . and toast!

On the other hand, men's shoes? Black and brown! And sadly, tragically, for men, one choice too many. Because he still has to turn to his wife and say, "Honey, which one should I wear tonight? Huh? I got black and brown here, and . . . please . . . help me out . . . I swear this'll bust a guy's brain. How do you do it?"

But for the true depth of female color intricacy, nothing in my experience tops what a woman said to me one night after a standup show. Having heard me reel off that long, long list of shoe colors, this gentle woman tracked me down and said while that may have been impressive, "You forgot seafoam."

She was right. And I was floored!

And to any man not frightened by that level of intellect, you are a fool. This woman listened to a rapid-fire list of over 50 colors, and when it was over, she knew both which ones had been said and which had not. Any woman who can do that, I'm afraid of, and my fellow men should be, too.

But it doesn't stop there. Ever shop for makeup with a woman? There are over 4,000 different makeup products in the average WalMart alone. And women know every single one of them!

Not that she uses them all - of course not. From the thousands, she has carefully selected fifteen to twenty that make up the trav-elling squad. But she's aware of them all, and she knows when new ones enter the market and old ones leave.

By contrast, men have two makeup options: shave, and don't shave. Not that women don't envy that. Most women think it'd be great to have it as easy as a man, just to be able to wake up on a Saturday morning, hop right out of bed, look straight in the mirror and proclaim, "I look great! Let's get outta here. C'mon, honey, we're burnin' daylight."

But most women can't do that, so have a little sympathy, men. Most women have to get up in the morning, confront the mirror, and start mixing chemicals!

And there are so many of them that they really need to know what they're doing. Because they've got eyeliner, lidliner, browliner, lipliner, blush, rouge, foundation, oily creams, non-oily creams, cold cream, wrinkle cream, face cream, hand cream, foot cream, day cream, night cream, creme rinse, mascara, lip shadow, lip gloss, lipstick . . . it's nearly endless.

Women actually have - are you ready for this? - moisturizer and dehydrator! Let that sink in. Moisturizer <u>AND</u> dehydrator. Apparently part of their body is a desert, and another part is a swamp! And it takes a serious land-management effort to keep it all in balance!

And the complexity of women's nails! There are over 1500 different products because women want to care for their nails. Some items to cut, shape, sharpen and hone; others to strengthen and fortify; others to decorate and adorn; and just in case everything fails, they can buy fake nails to glue on - and they will, because nails are simply that important. Nails serve a lot of important functions for women. They can be used offensively, defensively or erotically; they have utilitarian purposes like ripping and tearing; they can be used to brag to other women, and to lure men.

On the other hand, in a man's world, nails have but two purposes:

beer tabs and nose picking. It's sad to admit, but boogers-to-Budweiser pretty well sums men up! A simple world for simple beasts.

Rex Havens

Sometimes the lesson that your wife has to teach you is that there is no point in administering the lesson because, even with all your male powers plugged in and focused, you are not capable of mastering the material.

Such is the case with women's clothing and their alien size system.

I've tried, and I've seen other men try, but it's futile and hopeless. Sorry fellas, but from head to toe we're just not wired to understand this mysterious method women use to dress themselves.

It starts with the bra. Men can't even understand the everyday commercials we see on TV. For example, what happens if you wear an 18-hour-bra for about a week? Heaven only knows, but it can't be pretty.

That's how Sarah lets me know she's ready for a big day of shopping. She says, "Look out, honey, I put on my 18-hour-bra." I say, "I gotcha beat, got on my seven-day shorts! Popped 'em on Tuesday, still goin' strong!"

Also from the commercials, men don't know why a woman would even want a bra that will "lift and separate." Separate? Is that important? Tangled breasts a big problem for some women? Keeping them apart a big challenge? Are women really complaining to one another, "Will you just look at this mess!? I just washed 'em and I can't do anything with 'em. I would give my left one just to know which one is my left one. I've _got_ to get a filing system."

Even as boys, we males were confounded to learn that there was such a thing as a "training bra." What? Training? Apparently, we could only guess, when breasts are new they can be quite . . .

unruly? Perhaps, like a new puppy, one must "train" them to "stay." It must be like growing roses, we conclude, in that you have to make sure to start them correctly, or they might come in crooked.

And who was the evil scientist who devised the illogical A-thru-D cup size scale? Young boys attend school for years, striving to achieve, and it's deeply embedded into their heads that an "A" is a good thing and a "D" is a bad thing. Then, after years of learning and coming to understand that an "A" is better than a "B", which is better than a "C", which is better than a "D", along comes the bra world to say, "Time Out! New Rules. Everything you thought you knew is now exactly the opposite!"

Men have no experience with a scale where a D is better than an A. We're taught to shoot for A's, and to fear that a D might even be punishable! Bring home an A, everybody screams for joy, you get a steak dinner. Bring home a D, they just scream, no dinner.

But then about the age of 16, many of us are strangely attracted to the lure of breasts, so much so that we want to learn the language and everything else about them. And with this first exposure to the universe of female clothing sizes, men learn that nothing we know is relevant, the rules are totally random and arbitrary, and logic must be abandoned if this new system is ever to be absorbed. Because now men learn they are living in a world where one should be ashamed of a D in a classroom, but proud of a D in a sweater. And in fact, where sweaters are concerned, two D's are even better than one! But beware, three is a problem. You can have too much of a good thing.

Understand that men like to believe we are good at logic. Men believe they are able to take a problem and think it through to a cold, calm, logical, rational solution. And when it comes to men's clothing sizes, that is indeed the case. Men's clothing sizes make sense. It's a simple system, and one could explain it to someone easily and within minutes. If a man's jacket is size 44, that means he's 44 inches around the chest. Size 36 pants means he's 36 inches around the waist. If a dress shirt is size 16-35, that means he's 16 inches around the neck and 35 inches down the sleeve. Simple, logical, explainable.

Man #1: "What size does your wife wear?"

Man #2: "Daaah, I don't know for sure. I think it's either ten . . . or 'W.' But I think I've heard ten a few times, so I'm goin' with ten."

Man #1: "OK, ten what?"

Man #2: "Daaah . . . I really dunno. Uh . . . ten . . . wait, I can get this . . . gotta be somethin' simple, right, like ten . . . femimeters? Ten units of woman? Ten . . . lady pieces? I just know that a tiny little woman is a two, so I guess she's five times bigger than that? Does that sound right? No, probably not . . . and I'm sorry."

I found by asking hundreds of men that most believe size two is as low as her sizes get. Many men are surprised to learn there is actually a size one, and they're positively floored when they learn that below a one, there really is - drumroll, please - size ZERO! Try it at home. Drop that info on a man and watch his face. It's good, quality fun.

"Are you kiddin'? There's a ZERO?!?"

Yes, gentlemen, it is in fact the dream of some women to walk into a dress shop and say, "I'd like to see something in a nothing! I'm not a two, not a one. No, I'm a none! It's a curse, I can't help it, but I am just tooooo tiny for positive numbers."

And gents, in their dreamiest of dream worlds, they'd try on a zero . . . and it's too baggy! Now she needs something from the minus-negative part of the shop.

So abandon all loyalty to logic when the subject is women's clothing and her accessories. Women will actually buy and wear a tight little belt for the neck, which is blatantly and explicitly called - ready? - a CHOKER! No man would go near a device which tells you right up front that it's a "choker." To a man, a choker is a wrestling hold, and potentially fatal. It's so dangerous it's illegal, so you have the comfort of knowing that if your opponent uses it, he'll be disqualified, and you'll be declared the winner. Posthumously, but congratulations all the same. You added one to the wins column and the undertaker added one to the cemetery.

But women will voluntarily, and with their own hands, put something called a choker around their necks. Apparently the drive to accessorize is so strong that women are willing to risk oxygen-deprivation to achieve it. Is it possible that women endure this torture just to obtain the company of men? I asked Sarah, who suggested I consider the possibility that a little oxygen-deprivation makes the company of men more palatable.

Know also, men, that women hate it when we try to use logic against them in this area. For example, Sarah has started saying she wants a tennis bracelet. My reply, "I think we should get you a racket first! Let's see how you take to the game before we buy the uniform."

The lesson? Don't use logic. It can only end badly.

Chapter #14

- Female Football -
Civil Turf Wars Come Out Of The Closet

Rex Havens

Men, when we retreat into our little world of football, we think we're escaping to a place where women won't follow, because they don't understand, live and love the game like we do.

What men often fail to understand, to our detriment, is that women not only understand the concept behind football, but are masters of it. In fact, they use it against us every day.

This is because marriage is, and has always been, about ground-gaining and land acquisition. Two people, only one house. Can you feel the tension and suspense? Then let's suit up and get this bowl game under way!

The whistle to start the game blows the minute the new couple moves into their first residence. But the problem is it's on an extreme frequency well beyond the range of man-made instruments, which means only women can hear it. Therefore, the new husband is oblivious even to the fact that the game is underway. He's often at the concession stand looking for a brat and a beer, blissfully ignorant that she's racking up points against a defense that's not even on the field. Heck, you don't even need to be a good player to score against an opponent who hasn't even pulled his jock on, right!?

Make no mistake, gentlemen, your house in an ongoing gridiron battle, whether you recognize it or not. That's because the object of both marriage and football lies in fighting for, claiming and occupying your opponent's territory. When a wife "gains ground", it's around the house, not on the football field, but it's every bit as hard-fought and competitive, the result of careful planning, practice and execution. Like every great competitor, she analyzes her opponent's strengths (right!) and weaknesses, learns his patterns and habits, then pounces when he least expects it and where he is the most poorly defended. And once she acquires a piece of territory, look out, because she never, never, never, never, NEVER gives it back!!

Sarah is the perfect example. She's resourceful, savvy, ruthless, shrewd, and can map out a game plan to rival Lombardi, Shula and Noll combined. Sarah actually took a beautiful, spacious, huge his-and-her walk-in closet and converted it . . . to a HER! This closet is bigger than my first apartment, and not one thing in there is mine! This is a room that should be adequate to house clothing for ten and still have space left over for a grand piano and a chest freezer. But not so much as one sock in that suite belongs to me.

That's something about men that fascinates me endlessly, that a man can maintain his illusion of superiority when she's annexed the entire closet, while he's left with two doorknobs on the guest room. Or his stuff's in a refrigerator crate down by the furnace. He's changing clothes on a cold concrete floor, still muttering to himself, "But I'm the king of this castle, by golly!" Sure you are, Captain Delusion!

Closet displacement is usually the first place that the new husband realizes he's being pushed around like so much furniture, but it's far from the last. Quietly and gradually, Sarah has taken over most of the square footage of our house.

Know this, new husbands:

Your wife is there primarily to colonize the house.

Wives are like pilgrims. They arrive, smile, show courtesy and bring food. They seem friendly enough. But make no mistake, they have an unspoken agenda. Eventually they acquire one piece of territory, then another, then another, until the husband is pushed off onto a tiny, primitive, comfortless, resource-starved reservation known as the garage.

Inside one year of marriage, new husbands, know and expect that the garage will be all you'll have left of your "kingdom." Her part of the house has carpet, curtains, potpourri, grace, ambience, mood lighting and lace. Your part doesn't even have drywall or heat!

And when the husband is in her part of the house, there's still the question of decorating. This is yet another language men cannot decode. The reason, I learned, is because men are deaf. It turns out a house also makes sounds only a woman can hear, just like the whistle that started the game he doesn't know he's in.

Houses, I now understand, speak to women. Houses do not speak to men.

I first became aware of this one day when I arrived home to find we had an entire brand new dining room set. Thousands of dollars I would not have spent, but that's because I'm deaf.

Because Sarah informed me that in fact the house was, in her words, "screaming" for new dining room furniture. Screaming? I said, "Our house was screaming?" Apparently our house belongs in a Steven King novel. I asked, "Why didn't I hear all the screaming?" Sarah said she didn't know, but fortunately, she heard it distinctly enough for both of us. And fortunately, with the purchase of this furniture, she had made the house happy again and, for the moment, the house had stopped screaming.

She explained that houses scream for things when they detect that the overall composition of the domestic landscape is out of balance. One house might scream for a new sunroom, another for designer drapes, and yet another for a remodeled bathroom.

Sarah assured me that houses only scream when absolutely necessary, and they are to be heeded. Our house was screaming
because our old dining room set no longer fit in. I scream, you
scream, homes scream for the Broyhill team!

Naturally, I had to ask, if the house was screaming so loud, why
hadn't someone else heard it? Surely a neighbor, the mailman, a
pedestrian, someone would have heard the horrible screaming and
brought it to my attention, if only to reestablish peace and quiet in
the neighborhood. Sarah said that, indeed, other WIVES were
aware of the screaming, and they had collaborated on a team
effort to get the house what it needed so it could be at peace
again. For the time being, I was told, my house was not screaming for anything. Not that I would know, because to my ears it
turns out that a happy house and a screaming house sound exactly alike. But my wife has told me not to worry about it, because
she and her friends will take prompt action when - not if - the
screaming returns.

So decorating is best left to the wife, because men just do not
speak the language. But a warning to new husbands, even if you
want to be part of a decorating decision, be prepared to be
ignored and defeated. In fact, all your participation can realistical-
ly achieve is to slow down the process.

On those rare occasions when I do visit the furniture store with
Sarah, we never agree on what to get. I tend to pick louder,
more flamboyant pieces, as do many men, I have been told. But
Sarah always tells me we should go with more conservative items,
often in "earth tones." Again the language barrier rears its ugly
head. "Earth tones?", I ask. "You mean, like dirt? When I have
earth tones on my shoes, you won't let me in the house! Now all
of a sudden we're going to drop big money for colors we pay
Stanley Steemer to remove?"

But Sarah will hear none of it, opting for earth tones, and explaining to me that we shouldn't get my louder, brassier choice because, in her words, "We'd get tired of it." To which I respond, once again failing to think, "Great. Let's get what you want, and we can be tired of it instantly! My way, at least we get a month of fun. With earth tones, we don't even get that, because they left the color and fun out of it at the factory."

The session ends, cash registers ring, I wave good-bye to the chair I wanted, and we go home to wait for the delivery truck to bring us more earth tones.

That home may be your castle, fella. But it's her canvas, and you don't get a brush.

Chapter #15

A Rose, By Any Other Name, Can Make It All Right Again

Rex Havens

Every man in the history of men has screwed up and needs to know what to do to get back in her good graces and beyond. (Let's face it, "beyond" is important, because good graces may be nice, but they don't curl your toes and make you forget your own name. Men don't want only to be forgiven. They're hoping to make it to the great "beyond.")

You might think there are some men so virtuous, considerate and thoughtful that they've never blundered into the "Land of the Unforgiven." Men who've never had to dirty their knees begging for redemption. Mythical, godlike men who never had to beg for mercy in Her Highness's Court.

But you'd be wrong!

Every man - repeat, every man! - has either found or will find himself in that position, no matter how gracious his demeanor might seem. Phil Donahue? Sure. Alan Alda? No question. Paul Newman? Are you kidding? Mr. Newman, by his own account, when he was 80 years old, bummed cigarettes from an extra on a movie set, then was quoted as saying, "Can you do me a favor? Don't tell my wife you gave these to me." Butch Cassidy wouldn't be afraid of a woman if he wasn't haunted by bad experiences from crossing her in the past! And if woman can scare Butch Cassidy, then honestly, what chance do you have?

So certain is it that every man will eventually find himself on her bad side that Hallmark has pre-written an entire series of cards for when - not if - it happens. Hallmark literally bets on the fallibility of man, and prepares a product the male offender can buy when - not if - the offense occurs.

Hallmark is cocked, loaded and ready to profit from each and every male who makes a wrong move. If no man screws up,

Hallmark would have to eat all those cards. They'd lose a bundle. But instead they're poised to make - and do make - a fortune because you cannot lose betting against good collective male behavior.

Hallmark's biggest annual sales event, of course, is Valentine's Day, named after the Roman priest who, around 270 A.D., defied Emperor Claudius the Second and performed marriage ceremonies despite the fact Claudius had outlawed them. Claudius was not amused, and Valentine eventually lost 10 inches of stature which had previously been his head. But what Valentine lacked in height he made up for in holiness, became a saint, and centuries later we continue to celebrate his brave acts in furtherance of sweet love every February 14.

Which, I believe, raises the need for a new Hallmark holiday on February 13. It turns out many men today use Valentine's Day as a general apology day for any sins committed in the weeks or months leading up to the day. As a result, many men find them-selves in a goodwill deficit position coming into Valentine's Day, and use their gifts and cards on February 14 just to get back to even. And if one has only made it back to even, it can be difficult to attain the "beyond."

Therefore, I propose that February 13 should be National "I'm Sorry" Day. This would be a countrywide, CARD-ONLY day of male atonement, when forgiveness is sought for anything which might dampen the mood on Valentine's Day proper. No gifts!! They come the next day, always have, and it's expensive enough the way it is! February 13 would be a $4.95 occasion at most, with the emphasis not on the material, but the emotional compo-nent of being cleansed, renewed, refreshed, redeemed and forgiv-en.

Yes, I can hear some of the women crying, "What? No gift?

What kind of a romantic holiday comes with no gift?" Ladies. Please. Can't you wait just 24 hours? Just one more sunrise? One lousy rotation of the Earth. St. Valentine didn't defy Rome and die in vain. Gifts will come tomorrow. Do you know how close that is? It's already tomorrow in Japan. Please, think of it as one more card than you otherwise were going to get this year, accept his gesture and apology, erase the ledger, reset his account to zero, and hit February 14th with spirits high. And if the night of the 14th gets here and he still hasn't come through, there'll still be plenty of time to plan his painful and torturous demise.

But even if we successfully establish this new holiday, no single national day of "Sorry" will eliminate the need for men to continue apologizing from time to time. Some mistakes are so big they can't be put on the shelf to fester until next February. Some mistakes must be apologized for . . . and NOW! Otherwise he might not make it to next February.

So men will always need to know how to apologize, and they should be prepared to act quickly and in the most appropriate and effective way.

In my standup career, I have asked many audiences, "When a husband messes up, traditionally, what should he buy for his wife as an apology gift?" The overwhelmingly majority answer is always flowers. Yes, a few say diamonds, but we're talking working people here, so flowers it is. Sometimes I follow up and ask, "If it's flowers, then specifically, what kind of flowers?" And always the loud, *unanimous* voice of every crowd cries back, "Roses."

It's a jarringly simple voice to hear. There is never any dissent. Diverse audiences, from all over the country, sometimes from all over the world, vastly different walks of life, and with no preparation or rehearsal, they thunder out with a forceful, authoritative, single voice, "Roses!"

It's as though they're saying, "Hey, we're not stupid. We know the score. You go to the store, you get roses, you go home, hold 'em out, and you say, 'I'm sorry!'"

That is in fact why there are over 30,000 flower shops in the U.S. Three reasons, really. Weddings, funerals and "I'm sorry!"

But ask an audience, on the other hand, "When a wife wishes to apologize to her husband, traditionally, what should she buy for him?" and a most awkward yet amused silence falls over a crowd. Give them more time, lots more time, but still no answer will come. Then finally the magical music of laughter when they're asked, "Do you feel the confusion?"

The laughter flows freely then. Because they recognize, based on the reality their own lives, that there is no traditional gift for a wife who has messed up to buy for her husband. And why not? Because women don't mess up often enough for there to be a tradition!

To have a tradition, one must have frequency, meaning it must happen a lot. Men screw up constantly, and we have developed roses as our tradition. The average woman only messes up 3-4 times in her whole life (I think it's in the by-laws), and that is not enough for a tradition to take root.

An unexpected by-product of this line of inquiry is that women will regularly respond with, "No, you don't _buy_ him anything. You know what you do!!" Which is said while rolling the eyes seductively to indicate that wifely apologizing involves activity above and "beyond."

To which I can only say: Fellas, stop and think about that concept, if you can possibly get your head around it. Sex . . . as an APOLOGY!?!?! Stunning. Truly stunning. Women, all we men want to know is how did you get there? And when can we men ever hope to catch up?

When can we men hope for the day when we can come to you and say, "Sweetheart? I just feel so bad about what I did. All I want in the world is for you to forgive me. And, well, if you have to . . . TAKE ME NOW! Show no mercy, honey, I was bad, MAKE ME SORRY!!"

Don't hold your breath, fellas.

Rex Havens

Men and women. So what does it all boil down to? What do I think I've learned about men and women from fifty-four trips around the sun? Just this.

Men love efficiency.

Women love beauty.

I hear you. "Really? That's it? The whole thing is that simple? Come on! After all the millions of years of human gender interaction, it all comes down to efficiency versus beauty?"

To which I can only reply that it does not explain everything, only most of what's important. Please, take a little ride with me, and see if you agree.

First, men are motivated by efficiency because most men's lives are, indeed, a quest for ever-greater efficiency. In many households, even as we grow from boys into men, it's our job to get things done. Most men grow up being expected to build, repair, mend, adjust, fix, rig, restore, wire, patch and paint things. It's our job, often not a fun one, but a role we're expected to fulfill before we can move on to our favorite pursuits - recreation and leisure.

But in order to goof off, men are first expected to produce helpful results around the castle. So, naturally, men are attracted and motivated by any machine or device which hastens those results and speeds him on his way to the lake, ballpark, race track, arena, pub, stadium or golf course. Men get excited by devices that do what they say they will and do them quickly with no wasted time or motion. It's not that men enjoy the chore, but more that men crave the moment when the chore is done.

Women, on the other hand, while they may appreciate efficiency, are inspired more by beauty and things which feed the soul. That is the only possible explanation why, in this day and age, one can still find candle stores.

There is not a man alive who understands why there are still candles for sale, let alone why there are entire stores - thousands of them! - whose sole inventory consists of candles. To a man's utilitarian mind, candles in this day and age simply make no sense. Candles are unnecessary in a modern world. They have been far surpassed in efficiency by more recent strokes of genius.

A modern light bulb may have the light of a thousand candles. In fact, that's how the brightness of light bulbs is measured and expressed - in "candle power." A modern furnace has the heat of a million candles. Wow! To a man's way of thinking, with efficiency like that available, why would anyone ever choose to fool around with one candle at a time? Men don't understand why something whose useful time has passed has not gone the way of the buggy whip.

But women have patiently explained to me that they value the beauty, aroma, atmosphere, aura, even the soul of a single, burning candle. And that is why candle stores still exist, and that is Sarah's place at the mall.

My place is the bench in the middle of the mall.

The mall bench, of course, is where husbands sit with all the other husbands. There's never been a woman sitting on the mall bench with us. It's just one, big, sit-down stag party. It's the mall's version of limbo, an arid no-woman's land, and should probably be officially named the "Bored Captive Husbands Day Care Center." Just for variety, it would surely be fun someday to see one woman sitting on one mall bench somewhere in the USA, crying out,

"Fred's trying on pants, this could take all day!"

So there it is. Men prize efficiency, and women prize beauty. And you do not have to look any further to see these two competing philosophies living side by side than your standard, everyday bath towel.

It's hanging right there on the rod in your bathroom. Most of what there is to know about men and women, draped in plain view right there next to the sink.

Because your normal bath towel is composed of a male part and a female part. They exist side by side, each different but each making its contribution to the whole, finding a way to overcome obstacles and work together in peace for the common good.

The male portion of the towel, of course, is the big, fluffy terrycloth part in the center of the towel. This is the male part, naturally, because it is so remarkably efficient. This part of the towel is soft, thirsty, absorbent, and it literally sucks up the water. A person can dry oneself with the male portion of the towel. And that is what we men foolishly thought a towel was supposed to do!

But then there are the female portions of the towel. These are, of course, the decorative strips at each end of the towel. And to the women of the world, no matter how pretty you may think these additions are, even you must admit that these deco-bands are USELESS to the main purpose of the towel, which is, or at least should be, to eliminate moisture.

But that is not possible, because these flowery end pieces are hard . . . and flat . . . and matted . . . but most mysteriously, **they repel water!** What?? They're part of a towel. But they repel water! Lay the towel flat on a table and pour water on it.

The water will soak rapidly into the male part - and bead up on the female part! This is not just failure of a component to do its job, this is counter-efficient engineering intentionally inserted on the drawing board. To a man, this is a planned crash even before the opening flag!

Men simply do not know what to make of the deco-bands. If the whole towel was made out of this, it wouldn't be a towel - it would be a placemat. Would you want to try to dry yourself after a shower with a placemat? Probably not. Yet somewhere at the factory, they took two slices of placemat, and they sewed them into my towel!

To a man's way of thinking, this part of the towel has no business being part of a towel. It would be like having underwear made out of mostly cotton, but a little ice cream.

Women say, "But they're decorative towels." But men think those two words should not be allowed to appear together. Men believe there should be towels, and there should be decorations, but the two should never be combined.

And far from just being inefficient, these deco-bands can actually hurt. You can nick yourself with this part of the towel. So gentle-men, next time you're drying with the family linens and these nasty strips of sandpaper scrape you in a sensitive area, just think of it as a friendly little "hello" from your wife, offered in the name of art, and for the sake of beauty.

Men ask why fully 20% of every towel must be sacrificed so there can be beauty in the bathroom. To a man, this is valuable towel area that we could use to get 20% dryer, 20% faster. And that is important to men *because most of us are at least 20% bigger!*

Men would say, if there must be beauty in the bathroom near the towel rod, please ladies, by all means, buy a painting. Hang it on the wall right above the rod on which hangs a 100% plain terry-cloth towel. Then literally everyone would be happy. Visitors to your bathroom would have beauty when they look in that direction, and your husband would not resent the painting because he would not have to dry himself with it!

Gentlemen of the world, if we decided to unite, we could mount a campaign and try to get rid of the irrational decorative towel strip. We could use logic and reason and try to win women over and eliminate this inefficient little demon. I campaigned for male causes with the women in my life when I was totally, absolutely, thoroughly, hopelessly young. I was naive, I was idealistic, but mostly I was fatally young.

Yes, I was a young man once. But, like I said, it didn't work out.

But I fought hard for male causes. I fought valiantly with my Sarah, at least I thought I did. But in the end I had to admit I seldom won her over to my way of thinking. She is a formidable adversary, as are most in her Sisterhood.

So, gentlemen, I say to you only that women are the reason for many, many things in the world, and I ask you to find it in your heart to appreciate, learn from, and even love what they bring to the table.

For there truly are so many fine and wondrous lessons you can learn from your wife.

For women are the reason for pumps and clogs and flats and slings, periwinkle and seafoam, size zero, candle stores and decorative linens. And they are the reason for millions of other both greater and lesser things, all of which add texture, interest, beauty, mystery and magic to the fabric of life.

So, gentlemen, when you're tempted to take these women on, and challenge the feminine influences in the world, but all means do what's in your heart. But my advice, use your head, save a lot of time, add literally years to your life, and about nine out of ten times, be a very wise man:

Throw in the towel!

I Almost Forgot

Always remember that communication is the key to a successful marriage. The experts say it so often it's become trite, but it's nonetheless true. Sometimes, gentlemen, you can go by what she says. Other times, you need to read between the lines. In my own case, recently I was standing in my kitchen, and Sarah came up behind me and grabbed me by the seat of the pants. And I thought, "Hey! That's gotta be a good thing."

Turns out my little darlin' was just drying her hands.

You see, fellas, that's what marriage is all about.

Sometimes it's your job to understand and make peace with the towel.

And other times it's your job to be the towel.

Rex Havens